W9-AUM-276

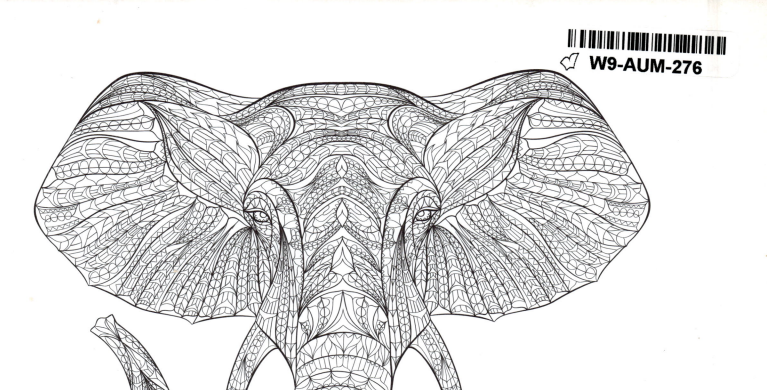

ANIMALS
NIGHT & DAY
COLORING BOOK

First edition for North America published in 2016 by Barron's Educational Series, Inc.

© Copyright 2016 by Carlton Publishing Group.

All rights reserved. No part of this publication may be reproduced or distributed
in any form or by any means without the written permission of the copyright owner.

All inquiries should be addressed to:
Barron's Educational Series, Inc.
250 Wireless Boulevard,
Hauppauge, New York 11788
www.barronseduc.com

ISBN: 978-1-4380-0897-4

Manufactured by: Leo Paper Group, Heshan, China

Printed in China

9 8 7 6 5

For best results, colored pencils are recommended.

Picture credits: Patricia Moffett and Shutterstock.com

AMAZING ANIMALS TO BRING TO LIFE

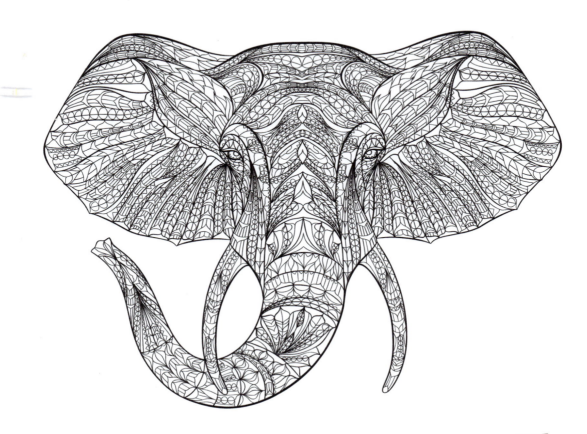

ANIMALS
NIGHT & DAY
COLORING BOOK

BARRON'S

CONTENTS

CARP

DEER

FROG

BOAR

LEMUR

BEAR

GIRAFFE

OTTER

PANDA

ANTELOPE

LION

HIPPO

PUG

DOVE

HYENA

BISON

TURTLE

WOMBAT

GOAT

SLOTH

FOX

BEAVER

PARROT

MEERKAT

SPHYNX

Introduction

Welcome to a new coloring challenge!

The *Animals Night & Day Coloring Book* is unique because it invites you to color not just against white, but also blue, black, and gold backgrounds. Each of the 90 detailed animal outlines featured here are displayed against both a day and a night backdrop, providing you with superb opportunities to highlight tone and texture, and create striking contrasts.

While daylight can illuminate subtle motifs and tints, darkness can bring out flashes of color or the sparkle of eyes and teeth. In fact, you'll find there's a surprising difference between an animal depicted in golden sunshine or azure seas and that same creature shown against a background of inky darkness or deep waters.

The animals presented in this book range from the domestic to the exotic. They include many favorites, such as the lion, koala, panda, meerkat, and elephant, as well as less familiar creatures, like the hyena, hippo, sloth, and bison. There are intricately patterned creatures, such as the giraffe and hummingbird, and nocturnal animals, including the owl, lemur, and racoon.

What was beautiful in the daytime can seem threatening at night, and what was subtle in the light can emerge from darkness as striking or even eerie. How will your daylight tiger differ from your midnight version? Could your drowsy daytime wolf become a moonlight predator? Might the lizard's camouflaged colors turn neon after dark?

How you decide to bring out the appearance, character, and qualities of each creature is determined by you and the color choices you make on each animal artwork. You can be as accurate and realistic, or as creative and fantasy-filled, as you like. Working with the colored backgrounds opens up exciting possibilities and an invigorating new world of coloring, so let your imagination—and your pens—run wild.